Praise for *Less Doing, More Living*

"I've seen many programs for improving lives (and created a few myself). Ari Meisel's philosophy in *Less Doing, More Living* is a true gem—simple, fun, and technologically up-to-date for the twenty-first century. This book will help you easily remove the stresses of day-to-day living and find that, in this removal, you'll have more time to enjoy the activities and people that you love."

> —DAVID BACH, #1 *NEW YORK TIMES*–BESTSELLING AUTHOR OF
> *THE AUTOMATIC MILLIONAIRE* AND *START LATE, FINISH RICH*

"*Less Doing* is an awesome book because it is a hands-on guide that teaches you how to quickly implement the art of 'strategic laziness'—doing only the most important stuff, and doing it well enough to get what you want. The stuff in this book will help you kick more ass, whether you're an entrepreneur, a student, or anywhere in between."

> —DAVE ASPREY, FOUNDER OF BULLETPROOF EXECUTIVE

"Ari Meisel's book is a KISS read packed with tons of valuable insights and tools to simplify your life, streamline your tasks, and allow you to focus on the right things with the right tools."

> —MARK DIVINE, AUTHOR OF *THE WAY OF THE SEAL* AND *UNBEATABLE MIND*

"Ari Meisel's *Less Doing, More Living* is a fittingly efficient read designed to help you optimize your life per nine fundamental principles. I came away inspired to further streamline my workflow, declutter my (dreaded) paper inbox, and obliterate my to-do list thanks to a host of great tech tool and time strategy recommendations."

> —CHRISTINE KOH, CO-AUTHOR OF *MINIMALIST PARENTING*:
> *ENJOY MODERN FAMILY LIFE MORE BY DOING LESS*

"I'm going to send an automated reminder to myself to reread Ari Meisel's super-helpful book every month. It's got an absurd number of tips that make my life easier."

—A. J. JACOBS, FOUR-TIME *NEW YORK TIMES*–BESTSELLING AUTHOR

"This smart and practical work illustrates Meisel's approach to efficiency and effectiveness in all aspects of life. It's a road map of tools and tricks to help you be better at what you do in less time, regardless of your discipline, so that you can have more 'free' time to spend however you like."

—SEAMUS MULLEN, AWARD-WINNING CHEF, RESTAURATEUR, AND COOKBOOK AUTHOR

"Efficiency is a lost art nowadays, and Ari Meisel has armed you with an effective tool for increasing productivity in the midst of the chaos. Every aspect of your life can become better with just a few simple and implementable changes that you'll be shocked by how easy they are to do. Free yourself to do what you were meant to do so you can live the way you want to live. Start doing less and living more today!"

—JIMMY MOORE, AUTHOR OF *CHOLESTEROL CLARITY: WHAT THE HDL IS WRONG WITH MY NUMBERS?*

LESS
DOING

MORE
LIVING

TARCHER/PENGUIN
a member of Penguin Group (USA)
NEW YORK

LESS DOING

MORE LIVING

Make Everything in Life *Easier*

Ari Meisel

BELLEVILLE PUBLIC LIBRARY

JEREMY P. TARCHER/PENGUIN
Published by the Penguin Group
Penguin Group (USA) LLC
375 Hudson Street
New York, New York 10014

USA · Canada · UK · Ireland · Australia
New Zealand · India · South Africa · China

penguin.com
A Penguin Random House Company

Copyright © 2014 by Ari Meisel
Penguin supports copyright. Copyright fuels creativity, encourages diverse voices, promotes free speech, and creates a vibrant culture. Thank you for buying an authorized edition of this book and for complying with copyright laws by not reproducing, scanning, or distributing any part of it in any form without permission. You are supporting writers and allowing Penguin to continue to publish books for every reader.

Most Tarcher/Penguin books are available at special quantity discounts for bulk purchase for sales promotions, premiums, fund-raising, and educational needs. Special books or book excerpts also can be created to fit specific needs. For details, write: Special.Markets@us.penguingroup.com.

Library of Congress Cataloging-in-Publication Data

Meisel, Ari.
    Less doing, more living : make everything in life easier / Ari Meisel.
        p.   cm.
    ISBN 978-0-399-16852-9 (pbk.)
1. Life skills.   2. Time management.   3. Stress management.   I. Title.
    HQ2037.M45   2014   2013042587
    646.7–dc23

Printed in the United States of America
10   9   8   7   6   5   4   3

BOOK DESIGN BY EMILY S. HERRICK

For my three sons, Benjamin, Sebastien, and Lucas,
who make me want to do better every day.

And for my wife, Anna,
sans toi je suis comme un navire sans capitaine.

Contents

Introduction

Welcome to *Less Doing, More Living*! I'm Ari Meisel. Before we begin, I'd like to give you a little background on me and on my "Less Doing" philosophy.

I've been an entrepreneur for most of my life. I started my first company at the age of twelve, doing website design. By the time I started college, I had also started a few other tech companies and, after college, I started working in construction.

When I visited a friend in upstate New York, I got the idea of creating a loft district in Binghamton. I spent the next three years working in construction. I built the lofts, a bar, and a few other spaces. Then I returned to New York City, where I started specializing in green building materials. I've invented two green building materials, written a book on green building materials, and spent most of the last eight years building and consulting.

In 2006, I was diagnosed with Crohn's disease, a very painful and incurable inflammatory disease of the digestive tract. My case was severe. I was in and out of the hospital, and I was taking sixteen pills a day. I nearly died.

After reaching a personal low point in the hospital, I decided to do everything in my power to strengthen my body, which by then was very weak. Through a combination of yoga, nutrition, natural supplements, and rigorous exercise like Ironman and CrossFit, I was able to fight back the symptoms of Crohn's until I was finally able to suspend my medication. Eventually, I was declared free of all traces of the "incurable" disease, and I completed Ironman France in June 2011 in thirteen hours and forty-five minutes.

I have since spoken at seminars and at a regional TED Talk about my struggle against a seemingly insurmountable opponent. What I discovered is that nutrition and fitness are not the whole story. Even with those things under control, stress was still a big part of my illness. It's a big part of many other autoimmune illnesses and inflammatory conditions, too, not to mention life in general. So before I could completely solve my problem, I needed a way to address stress.

Through the process of data collection, self-tracking, and analysis, I became an Achievement Architect, a coaching service that I've developed through a long process of experimentation, analytics, and personal tracking. Less Doing is my approach to dealing with the daily stresses of life by optimizing, automating, and outsourcing all of my tasks in life and business. Now I'd like to share that gift with you.

WHAT IS LESS DOING?

The idea of Less Doing is to reclaim your time and—more important—your mind, so you can do the things you want to do. Even little bits of time are important. It all adds up. By applying the practice of Less Doing to your life, you can free up the time and mental space to do the things you care about most.

The three keys to Less Doing are:

- Optimize

- Automate

- Outsource

These keys apply to health, productivity, or any other type of problem or goal.

For any challenge, the first thing to do is optimize it. Break it down to its bare minimum, simplify it, and eliminate everything that's not completely necessary. Once you've boiled the task down to its essentials, the goal is to break what's left into bite-sized tasks that can be replicated and possibly delegated.

After you've optimized a task, the next step is to automate as much as possible. Use software or processes so you can get the task done without human involvement—just set it and forget it.

Finally, for anything that's left, outsource to a generalist or a specialist. It's important to note that although outsourcing can do a lot for you, it comes *after* optimizing and automating. If you outsource an inefficient task, that doesn't really help because it's still inefficient. It's much better to eliminate work by optimizing or automating whenever you can and only outsource what's left.

I based the system of Less Doing on nine fundamental principles:

- The 80/20 Rule

- Creating an "External Brain"

- Customization

- Choose Your Own Workweek

- Stop Running Errands

- Finances

- Organization

- Batching

- Wellness

This book will lead you on a step-by-step journey toward making everything in your life easier. If you need more help, I invite you to take advantage of the resources at the end of the book, where I list links and websites to the apps and products mentioned in the text.

Thank you for joining me on this journey. Let's get started.

FUNDAMENTAL 1

The 80/20

Rule

T he idea of Less Doing is to reclaim your time and, more important, your mind. The 80/20 Rule is a great place to start.

You may have heard of the 80/20 Rule from Tim Ferriss. It's also called "the Pareto Principle." Italian economist Vilfredo Pareto developed this principle in the early 1900s, when he realized that 20 percent of the pea plants in his garden produced 80 percent of his pea crop. The same principle applies to many areas of life:

- 80 percent of the consequences flow from 20 percent of the causes.

- 80 percent of the results come from 20 percent of the effort and time.

- 80 percent of company profits come from 20 percent of the products and customers.

- 80 percent of all stock market gains are realized by 20 percent of the investors and 20 percent of an individual portfolio.

This is a formula you can apply to energy and resource allocation in your life. In the case of work, the work you do is a resource, and you probably spend 80 percent of your time on 20 percent of your clients or projects.

We only have so much time, and if you want to be successful without spending all day working, then you have to learn to work smarter. A huge part of this is focusing on the items that have a large return.

But how do you know where you need to focus? How do you know which areas of your life are yielding high returns?

That's where tracking comes in. Tracking is crucial because if you don't track—or measure—what you're doing, you can't make it better. In everything we do, something can be tracked, whether it's our health, the hours we spend on e-mail and Facebook, travel, or anything else. If we can figure out the elements required for the processes we do regularly, we can track them.

This is important because we have so many things going on in our lives that it's really easy to lose track of how we're actually spending our time. By six thirty p.m., a lot of people can't even tell you what they had for breakfast that morning, let alone which activities yielded the highest returns or what they need to focus on tomorrow.

TRACKING FOR RESULTS

There are many tools that can help you track various aspects of your life. The first step is to consider a key area of your life and think about how it could be measured. For example, if you want to improve your health, you might use food journaling, tracking your weight each day, or using a life-tracking device like Fitbit, which tracks your daily steps, distance, calories burned, and sleep.

For tracking productivity, here are several great tools:

- RescueTime: Tracks what you're spending time on when you're using a computer. It can show you which websites and applications you used and how much time you spent on them. It also has a feature that will allow you to voluntarily block distracting sites so you can't get to them and waste time.

- iDoneThis.com: Sends you an e-mail each evening asking what you got done that day. You tell it, in an e-mail reply. Even if you never look at that e-mail again, just writing down what you did at the end of the day has a measurable psychological effect on your productivity. It allows you to offload that information from your brain and stop thinking about it. On top of that, you can also share your updates with a team. You can use iDoneThis to keep your team up to date on everyone's progress, share results, respond, and comment. Another cool feature is that, after you use it for a while, iDoneThis starts periodically sending you an e-mail telling you what you did on a random day in the past. This can be fascinating—an e-mail might arrive about a project that you started three months ago and just finished that day.

- InsideTracker: You can even go so far as to track the biomarkers in your blood. This is different from doing it with your doctor, because you can test yourself whenever you want to, and many times doctors won't test for some of the markers offered by InsideTracker—such as C-Reactive Protein, an inflammatory marker. Tracking your vitamin D levels, cholesterol, and even testosterone allow you to dial in to your health and achieve better results.

Apply tracking and analysis wherever you can. You can always find a way to make things better, because there's always room for more efficiency.

OPTIMIZING YOUR PROCESSES AND CREATING THE "MANUAL OF YOU"

Once you understand how you spend your time, you can optimize the processes in your life. For an example of an optimized process, think about IKEA's product assembly manuals. To help customers build each product, IKEA has broken down the process into a set of instructions that is language-independent, requires as few steps as possible, and is (for the most part) fail-proof. The goal with your daily processes should be exactly the same. You need to break each process down to the fewest, most explicit steps possible so that they are easy for you to complete and, more important, can be automated or outsourced entirely.

Processes?

We all have processes that we complete on a regular basis: checking e-mail, writing reports, conducting research, generating content, reviewing materials, and making meals, among many others. These are things we do on a daily or weekly basis, or even just once in a while.

Most of these activities are routine. We can do them without even thinking, almost as if on autopilot. While this might seem like a good thing, the truth is if you can get these things done on autopilot, someone else could, too. It's easy to fall into a trap where we think we're the only ones who can do the things that make our worlds spin. But have we ever stopped to consider the steps we actually take?

As an exercise, think about something you do often. Now describe, on a very granular level, each step you go through to complete that activity. Think about it as if you were creating the "Manual of You," and you were going to give it to someone who doesn't know you or how you work. This person will have to complete the task without your help. This process can (and should) be applied to most of the things you spend your time doing.

I have clients complete this exercise with both incredibly complex tasks and very simple ones, with the same result: the perfect instruction manual. One client began with a process that was ten pages long. By the end of our work, he had a process with eleven easy-to-follow steps.

A personal example involves providing a discount code for one of my Skillshare classes to a potential student. If someone can't make it to a session they've paid for, I have my assistant generate a code so that the student can sign up for a future class free of cost. The process looked like this:

1. Go to www.skillshare.com.

2. Log in using user name ****** and password *******.

3. Go to "Dashboard" at the top of the page.

4. On the left-hand side, you will see "Upcoming Classes." Hover over the date of the specified class and hit "Manage." (It should pop up in orange.)

5. On the right-hand side, you will see discount codes. Choose "Create new code," and a little box will pop up.

6. You then choose the name of the code, which can be whatever you want (example: for August 15, I would title it AUG15).

7. Next, put in the appropriate discount and the number of codes you would like to create. Then hit "Create."

8. You will want to note the URL of the page you are on, because that is what you will send in the e-mail with the code for where to sign up.

9. Finally, e-mail the code with instructions to the person on the original e-mail.

The first time I wrote this, I left out step three, and the whole process had sixteen steps instead of the current nine. After I initially created the sixteen steps, I reviewed them and found immediate redundancies to remove. Then, the first time I sent the task off to a Fancy Hands assistant, he quickly pointed out that he didn't know where the "Upcoming Classes" link was found. This prompted me to realize I had glossed over the step explaining to go to the Dashboard first, so I added it.

The second time I sent it off, I got a different person (and hence a different perspective, since Fancy Hands is an on-demand assistant service). She pointed out superfluous aspects of some of the latter steps. I was able to whittle the process down further, to its current nine steps.

It's also important to get in the mind-set of "If This, Then That." Ideally, you want little or no communication between the time you assign a task and the time you get confirmation that the task has been successfully completed. So you must anticipate problems or forks in the road. In the task on the previous page, I might have added a line that read, "If more than one upcoming class date exists, provide a discount code for all dates," to avoid the question: "Which date did you want the code for?"

This might mean that you add an additional step for situations that come up infrequently. You only have to write it once, however, and it will save you from having to take the time to deal with it down the road. The point of all this is that, in the end, I was able to break this task down to an incredibly efficient, error-proof process that *anyone* can follow and complete.

Once a process has been perfected, delegate the task out of your sight and out of your mind. It's the first step to making life as easy as can be.

A NOTE ON ESSENTIAL VS. OPTIONAL

While I do focus on trimming the fat and paring things down to their most basic and efficient elements, that does not mean I don't enjoy the optional things in life.

As a matter of fact, the entire framework of "optimize, automate, and out-source" is meant to free up your time and your mind so that you can do the things you really want to and not just the things you have to. If the principles of Less Doing help you create an extra thirty minutes in your workday and you feel like spending this time on Facebook, by all means, eat your heart out. My mission is simply to make it so that you never feel guilty about doing the things you want to do because you "should" be doing something else.

To achieve that, you need to be able to separate the *essential* from the *op-tional*. Let's apply this to a personal situation of mine: blog reading. I follow over a hundred and fifty blogs and power through over a thousand news items each day. Why? Because I love to be in the know on the latest trends, coolest gadgets, and latest psychological studies on productivity. When I meet with my Achievement Architecture clients and they ask for software recommendations, odds are one of my blogs covered it and I can retrieve the answer. How can I possibly get through all these feeds each day? By making sure I cover the essentials and, if I have time (which I always do, thanks to Less Doing), working my way through the optional stuff while making phone calls or watching TV. "Optional," by definition, means "available to be chosen but not obligatory"— it's important to treat it that way.

Here's how it works for me. Each morning, I pull up my RSS reader (a program used to read news feeds) on my iPhone. (I like feedly, an app available for iPhone, because it syncs with my iPad.) If there are two hundred new items, there will usually be twenty essentials. I can read these essentials, post them to my blog, tweet them, and e-mail them to people I think would be interested, all while walking my dog for fifteen minutes. Then, throughout the day, I'll get through the other stuff. But if for some reason I can't, I know that I'm not missing any of the essentials. This gives me real peace of mind.

In feedly it's very easy to organize feeds into folders. Simply choose "Feed

Settings" and then add a check next to the folder you've created. Most RSS readers offer similar functionality.

As usual, I like to be able to translate these principles to other things like e-mail, errands (though you should never run errands), and even nutrition. Don't overcomplicate your life by creating so many boxes and organization systems that getting through the system is a chore in itself. Two "boxes"—Essential and Optional—are all you need.

80/20 ADVANCED

Once you've applied tracking and used the information you learned to stream-line your processes and focus on the essential, you've gone a long way toward optimizing your life.

Once you've done that, you can change the proportion of energy you spend on work. Ultimately, 20 percent of your energy (not time, but energy) should be spent on work. Spend other the 80 percent on rest and self-improvement. This may seem counterintuitive, but by investing in rest and self-improvement, you reap benefits that make you far more efficient and feed your work. It's a self-supporting cycle.

Creating an "External Brain"

· ·

One of the most important things you can do to have a life of Less Doing is to have a system that allows you to find anything at any time. You need constant, universal, instant access to everything you know.

The old way is to try to keep it all in your head, but that approach is inefficient. The problem with trying to remember everything is that in doing so, you run out of space in your head to actually think about the task at hand. What's worse, it doesn't always work. Often, even if I try really hard to remember something, I still forget it.

Using your memory to store everything is stressful and unreliable. How many times have you chanted a phone number or other fact over and over in your head, trying to lock it in, only to forget it before you needed it? Instead, you can create an "external brain" that stores everything reliably, offers instant access, and frees your mind for more interesting work.

The idea of an external brain comes from my experiences. In high school, I was getting a new business idea every week. Many were terrible, but I was writing them all down in a marble notebook. I had tons of ideas, and I'm pretty sure I invented a few things during that time.

In college, I got new ideas less frequently—maybe once a month—and after college, the ideas stopped altogether. I thought it was because I had gotten too old to have ideas anymore, figuring imagination must run out around age twenty. But if you look at my life at that time, I was working on construction sites eighteen to twenty hours a day and not allowing time for rest or recuperation. I couldn't think of new ideas—I simply didn't have the mental resources for that.

When I discovered Less Doing, it felt like a reawakening of my brain. I felt smarter, I could process things, and I started getting ideas again. By taking care of your brain and treating it as a precious resource, you build the foundation you need to be creative and do your best work. Using an external brain is a big part of that.

YOUR EXTERNAL BRAIN

The heart of the external brain is note-taking. If an idea is in your head, get it out. Ideas in your brain work like traffic on a highway: we have to create idea flow for good ideas to come out.

You may have seen the *Simpsons* episode where Mr. Burns goes to the Mayo Clinic and is diagnosed with everything, but even though he has every possible disease, the germs all block each other and prevent each other from killing him. To illustrate, the doctor shows Mr. Burns a doorway filled with fuzzy balls representing various forms of illness. None of the illnesses can get through the doorway because it's so crowded that they're all stuck.

Ideas behave in a similar way. You have to be able to get ideas into a single-file line so they can get out of your head. When you let your ideas flow freely, you get more ideas, and that leads to more good ideas.

Not all ideas are good—out of ten ideas, you may have eight that are bad or irrelevant. But even bad ideas can lead to good ideas. You want to get them out of your head not only because they may be blocking a good idea from coming out, but also because they may come together with some of your other ideas to make a good idea.

That's why, if you have an idea, trying to hold it in your mind is a problem. That's how we lose ideas.

SETTING UP YOUR EXTERNAL BRAIN

There are many great tools to help you capture information and ideas outside your head. My favorite app is Evernote.

Evernote

Evernote lets you take notes in any form: text, phone calls, pictures, drawings, scanned documents, web pages—you name it. You can tag things and organize them into notebooks within Evernote, or you can skip that and just find things by searching. That's what I do—Evernote's search feature is very effective.

Evernote is free, has no storage limits, and works everywhere. It syncs across the web, iPhone, Android, and desktop computers. This can be the heart of your external brain. If there's anything you want to remember, put it in Evernote. Put everything in Evernote and get it out of your head. The app is free—overuse it!

One great thing that makes Evernote even easier to use is an extension called Web Clipper. It works with Gmail, Chrome, and Firefox. If you view a website, an article, a video on YouTube—anything you want to remember—just click Web Clipper, and it will put it in Evernote for you.

That's great by itself. Even better, when you clip something, it will pop up any related items among the stuff you already have in Evernote. When you do a Google search, it also puts any related things from your Evernote at the top of your search results. This is where it becomes really fascinating. I have about eighteen hundred notes in my Evernote right now. (Seriously, overuse it!) Most of those notes may never be relevant or useful to me, but they're there, ready for me if I ever need them. This is the backup of my brain.

So, for example, let's say I'm doing some research for a blog post. I open up Google and search for the topic, and it reads, "You have three Evernote notes." Suddenly, my blog post research includes something I clipped a year ago, something from a few months ago, and something I clipped last week. All of these items, which may have seemed unimportant until now, are suddenly relevant, and here they are waiting for me. It's not just a regular Google search, it's something I had in mind and found interesting before, now recalled effortlessly.

It's incredibly liberating to have all that stuff there, ready and waiting for you, without worrying or trying to hold on to it or wasting effort trying to recall it later. It's literally like having a drop box for your brain.

It has been shown that Evernote works in a way that is very close to the way our brains work. Just as Pinterest has been described as "the way a woman's brain looks" (thus 73 percent of users are women), Evernote is the neuroscientist's model of how our brains organize information.

The only thing I know of that comes close to the functionality of Evernote is a memory technique called "mind loci." This is the technique used by competitors in the World Memory Championship, where the final event is to memorize the order of ten decks of cards. The amazing thing is, more than one person does this. You can just imagine if these guys got into an argument—they'd argue all day, each one convinced he remembers everything perfectly!

The mind loci technique works by visualizing putting memories and information into physical things. For example, if you asked me a question and I wanted to remember it, I might visualize putting it into the grand piano that's in the same room as me right now. Then, six months from now, I'd have to find my way back to this piano in my mind and find that piece of information. It's not easy to do, and it's not used often, but it is used by people in the legal profession or private investigators who need to remember the details of cases and situations.

Mind loci can work, but it's not a great use of your brain resources. Use Evernote instead.

AquaNotes

What about ideas you get in the shower? Studies have shown that we're most creative in a place where we're comfortable and warm. That's why so many people get ideas in bed and in the shower, and we've all tried to hold on to an idea by repeating it over and over. It never fails, though: the minute you open the shower curtain or door, you lose the idea. The problem is not only losing that idea, but also the frustration that comes with it. Frustration has resonating effects that make it harder to recover your creativity.

Here's another area where your external brain can take over. There's a waterproof Post-it pad called AquaNotes, specifically created so people can write ideas down in the shower.

FollowUp.cc

Another great service is FollowUp.cc. It's an automatic e-mail reminder service. All it does is send reminder e-mails, but the key is how you use it.

Here's how it works: I send an e-mail to someone. Let's say I want to remember to follow up with her in three days. This is exactly the sort of thing you don't need to waste mental energy keeping in your head. Instead, I add "3days@FollowUp.cc" to the BCC field. If the person hasn't responded in three days, FollowUp.cc will send me an e-mail reminder with a copy of the original e-mail and a snooze feature. You can set it for any time period you want: three days from now, a month from now, August 18 at nine p.m., every Friday. If you put the FollowUp.cc address in the BCC field, the reminder will come only to you. If you use the CC field, it also sends a copy of the reminder to the other person. In most situations, that's not what you want, but it can be helpful in certain situations.

For example, in a building where I teach, Verizon's FiOS service was supposed to be available. For three years, the Verizon website said it was available, but it wasn't. There's an e-mail address you can write to check on when FiOS will be available at a location, so I wrote to them and set up a one-day reminder using FollowUp.cc. In this case, I used the CC field instead of BCC, so they would get a copy of the reminder every day until they replied. Finally, after sixty-four days, someone wrote back, "Please stop your annoying reminder service. We don't know when service will be available in your building." I responded, "Why didn't you tell me that sixty-three days ago?"

This is incredibly powerful and liberating. Imagine how much energy I would have wasted if I had used only my own brain to get the same result! I encourage you to overuse these tools—there's no reason not to. About 80 percent of my e-mails go out with a FollowUp.cc, and there's one simple reason: five seconds after that e-mail goes out, it's gone from my mind. I don't have to think about it anymore, because I know it's taken care of. I can use those valuable brain resources for something better.

This also works for other situations. Say you meet someone at a party: "Let's catch up next week!" Someone goes on vacation: "Get back to me on August 26, when I'll be back in the office." No problem—just send an e-mail with a BCC to FollowUp.cc. The service also creates a calendar, so if you want to, you can look ahead and see all the follow-ups you have coming up. They could be from different times in the past, and they'll all get done on the right day. There's even a snooze function, so if a reminder comes in and it's not the right time, you can defer it until later.

IFTTT (If This, Then That)

An awesome service that I use to automate tasks is called IFTTT.com. The name stands for "if this, then that." IFTTT.com creates automations between any two web services. It includes YouTube, Twitter, Evernote, Google Calendar,

Delicious—all sorts of different services. The way it works is very simple: if *this* happens here, then *do that* over there. For example, if it's going to rain tomorrow, send me a text message. If I check in on Foursquare, put a note in Google Calendar.

I have it set up so that if I star an item in feedly, then it will get tweeted out, saved in an Evernote note (which I use at the end of the week to send out my "interesting things of the week" post), and added to Delicious, Zutual, and Storify to spread my social media reach. All these things happen through one action that I never have to think about again.

Contactually

For CRM (customer relationship management), there's a web service called Contactually. It will scan your e-mail and watch who you contact, who you follow up with, and who writes back to you. Using this information, it generates a list of five people each day that it suggests you contact. I don't know how they do it, but it's really good. For me, out of every five I get, three are people I look at and think, "Yeah, I really should contact that person." It's quite interesting.

Re:snooze

For reminders, there's Resnooze.com. This service will send you the same reminder on a repetitive interval, such as every two weeks or every month. Before I discovered this, I had a reminder in my calendar to give the dog a heartworm pill at nine a.m. on the first of every month. But I was usually doing something at nine a.m. on the first of the month, so I forgot about it and it didn't get done. Now it's in my inbox, and I have to deal with it before I can delete it.

HassleMe

Another reminder service is called HassleMe.co.uk. It's very similar, but it will send you the reminder on an approximate schedule instead of an exact one. For example, say you want to call your mom roughly every five days. You set this up in HassleMe.co.uk, and sometimes it will remind you after three days, sometimes after seven—a variable interval around the amount of time you specified.

The interesting thing about approximate intervals is that, for certain activities, the randomness actually helps you get it done. For example, say you want to get flowers for your girlfriend periodically. You really want to do it, but if you set a reminder every Thursday, it takes the sincerity out of it and makes it seem more like a chore. But if it comes up more randomly, it feels more genuine and the unpredictability makes it harder to brush off.

EMPTYING YOUR INBOX

E-mail inboxes can become a breeding ground for unfinished tasks, dread, and mental clutter. You can free a lot of mental resources by clearing out your inbox and keeping it empty.

The first step is to optimize and separate out the optional (nonessential) e-mails. Here is a fact: you only need two folders—Essential and Optional. Most of your e-mails are nonessential, so rather than looking at them at all, you can set up a filter to set them aside for you. With this one step, you can eliminate the majority of nonessential e-mails in the future, as well as messages currently in your inbox. This doesn't have to be complicated or daunting. All you need is the following filter:

Find any e-mail that *has* the term "Unsubscribe" and *doesn't have* the term "FW" or "RE," and put it in a folder labeled "Optional."

Any e-mail message with the option to unsubscribe from it is probably not an essential e-mail. These e-mails may well include some interesting information, but they don't require your immediate attention.

With an optimized inbox, everything there is something that should be dealt with, deleted, or deferred.

- If it's something you've already finished, delete it.

- If it's something you can do now, do it.

- If it's not something you can do now, defer it to a time that you can.

For the deferred tasks, you can use FollowUp.cc and its snooze function. For example, I might think Friday at ten a.m. will be the right time to do something. But come Friday at ten a.m., I'm busy. When the reminder e-mail comes in, I can hit snooze to push it off for an hour, a day, a week, or whatever unit of time I need to get to the right place where I can actually do it.

I realize that seems insanely simple, but the first step invokes the all-important Essential vs. Optional process. The second step is a skill set you need to develop. Over time you will get better and faster at "processing" e-mails. If you are a Gmail user, try "The Email Game" to work through these principles and get rewarded as you improve.

ELIMINATING YOUR TO-DO LIST

Your to-do list is destroying you! I'm adamantly and vehemently against all to-do lists of all kinds, whether it's Post-it notes, Wunderkit, Google Tasks, or worst of all, a whiteboard. The problem with the way most people use to-do lists is that they become a dumping ground for things that can't actually be done.

You're busy. You probably have dozens of items on your to-do lists. That's the problem. Most of these tasks require the input of someone else before you can do anything, and many more are long-term projects that you can't do anything about right now.

The worst to-do item I ever see on someone's list (and I see this all the time) is "write book." That's not a to-do; it's not even a goal. "Publish book" might be a goal, but "write book"? That's not a goal, and it's certainly not a to-do item. It's just too big. To give you an example of a good task, try "write one hundred words." That's optimized, it's repeatable, and it's manageable. You can do it in fifteen to twenty minutes and be done.

The problem with most to-do lists is that when you look at a list of forty things you have to do, including a number of things you can't do, all it does is remind you of what you're not getting done. That creates cognitive dissonance, which makes us subconsciously unhappy and unable to go forward. It enacts a verified psychological effect called the Zeigarnik effect. The Zeigarnik effect is a voice in our heads that pushes us to finish the unfinished. As human beings, we naturally want to finish things. Taken to an extreme, that's how we develop obsessive-compulsive disorder.

When we don't or can't finish the things we want to finish, it upsets us. If you think about evolution, this made sense back when cavemen basically had two things to do each day: eat and survive. But now we have phone calls to make and friends to talk to and TPS reports to file. It's hard to manage all those things in our brains at the same time. We need to clear out the noise.

You don't have to worry about to-do lists or prioritizing. All you need to do is work on your timing. Every task has a time associated with it: when it needs to be started, checked on, or finished. The idea is to bring those tasks into focus at the times you can actually deal with them—and then you deal with them. Then you never have to worry or think about them again.

That's where FollowUp.cc comes in. It allows you to replace your to-do list, using your e-mail inbox. Because it comes into your e-mail, and e-mail is a disruptive technology (unlike calendars and other reminder systems), you can use it to get rid of your to-do list completely.

To eliminate your to-do list, take an approach similar to dealing with e-mails.

Look at your current list and ask yourself this question: "When is the right day and time for me to do this item?" Then choose one of the following four options:

1. Do it now.

2. Defer it to the right time using FollowUp.cc. If it's a regularly recurring task, use Re:snooze. For approximate intervals, use HassleMe.co.uk.

3. Delegate it to your virtual assistant.

4. E-mail or manually add it to Evernote if it has to do with an idea, notes, or research.

For most items on your to-do list, the key is finding the right timing. Timing a task well isn't just about whether I'm busy or not busy—everybody has a different circadian rhythm. Just like there are morning people and night people and people who work out at different times, there are better times of day for each person to make phone calls, do meetings, and work. Now, obviously, we live in a world where we have to work with other people's schedules, but you want to do the best you can to work within the schedule that works best for you.

People often try to accomplish this with various calendars and reminder tools, but there's something special about e-mail. This disruptive technology is uniquely suited to getting us to do things. You've probably had the experience that when a calendar reminder pops up, you snooze it. Then you snooze it again, then again, then again. Then it's gone—and undone.

E-mail doesn't do that. If it's at the top of the list, it needs to be dealt with, deferred, or deleted. That's it. By processing e-mail this way and using FollowUp.cc to handle deferrals, you can keep your inbox clear and eliminate your to-do list. You can also replace most of the functionality of a CRM system, because you now have a system for handling follow-ups with customers and prospects.

After you eradicate your to-do list, you'll never need it again. Your inbox will become your de facto, extremely short-term and hyper-focused list of things that need to be done now—and that's all you need to be concerned with.

Once you get your e-mail optimized and handling your to-do list for you, the final piece of your external brain is a virtual assistant.

HIRING A VIRTUAL ASSISTANT

I believe everyone should work with a virtual assistant at some point. Whether or not you ever intend to work with an in-person assistant, working with a virtual assistant, or VA, is an educational process for you in terms of delegating.

Because you can get a VA for as little as twenty-five dollars a month now, there's no excuse not to try it.

Here's why hiring a VA is so valuable: if you can relay a task to someone you don't know and will probably never meet, that's the start of making your processes better. In the course of simplifying and explaining the task to the other person, you'll understand your process more clearly and develop a perfectly optimized task. As you do this for more tasks, you're effectively creating a "Manual of You" that you can use to transfer your tasks to other people without needing to rely on one specific person. It's well worth working with a virtual assistant, if for no other reason than to learn to optimize your processes this way.

How to Work with a Virtual Assistant

There are two kinds of virtual assistants: on-demand and dedicated. With on-demand assistants, there's a pool of assistants. One of them gets your task, does it, and moves on. You may never interact with that person again, and she knows nothing about you. With dedicated assistants, you deal with the same person every day, and he knows a lot about you and does a lot of things for you.

There are pros and cons to both. Personally, I use nondedicated, or on-demand, assistants. I've done extensive testing on twenty-three different VA

companies in the last three years, and I've found that the on-demand assistants are great for people who are just starting out and have few tasks, and
they're great for very advanced people. In the middle, you should be with a
dedicated assistant.

For virtual assistants, there are two companies I like to use.

- On-demand: Fancy Hands. Their service starts at twenty-five dollars a
  month for five tasks. For ninety-five dollars a month, you get unlimited
  tasks. They use all U.S.-based assistants.

- Dedicated: Zirtual. For $197 a month, you get a dedicated assistant and
  unlimited access, although the system tops out at ten hours. There are
  also more expensive plans that offer more hours per month. Again, the
  assistants are all U.S.-based. You always get the same person, so he
  or she gets to know you, your tasks, your e-mail, your habits, and your
  preferences.

It feels good to get to know one person and build a relationship, but in most
cases, you don't really need a dedicated assistant. Ninety-five percent of tasks

can be done by an on-demand assistant. The great thing about coming to this realization is that it makes you bombproof. You don't have to worry if something happens to the dedicated assistant you depend on. For example, I used to have a dedicated virtual assistant in India. She was very good, and I'd been working with her for over a year when suddenly she informed me that she was being promoted and would no longer be my assistant. After three days of sheer panic, I took a hard look at the tasks she had been performing for me. I realized that some were not necessary, the vast majority could be automated without human intervention, and the rest could be done by an on-demand assistant if I utilized the right tools.

The other great thing about using on-demand assistants is they're very scalable. If you send out a hundred tasks in one hour, a hundred on-demand assistants will do them in that hour, and you're still only paying ninety-five dollars a month. The on-demand assistants are 24/7, and with a hundred people working for you at once, the average turnaround time becomes about ten minutes.

I find that people have a lot of hesitation when it comes to using a virtual assistant, and price is usually not the issue. The two biggest concerns I hear from people are that they don't have the time to train someone new and that they don't know which tasks to have the assistant perform. But with plans starting at twenty-five dollars for five tasks, there's no excuse not to give it a try. You will be hooked, you will want more, and you will become more effective in the process. It's worth doing just for the training it will give you in streamlining your tasks and processes.

A "task" by Zirtual standards is anything taking up to twenty minutes. Can you imagine how efficient you would need to become to get most of your tasks done in less than twenty minutes? By communicating your ideas through e-mail, you naturally start to notice and eliminate inefficiencies. (This happens as you realize that steps two and four make no sense and steps six and seven are repetitive, for example.) Remember, we need to optimize before we do anything else. Getting a task down to its bare essentials makes it bombproof. If the majority of your tasks can be completed by someone who has no previous experience working with you, you're never at the mercy of an assistant who calls in sick or moves on to another company. It's like the virtual assistant version of Dropbox.

Since all the assistants at Zirtual and Fancy Hands are U.S.-based, their English is impeccable. I've had them call clients on numerous occasions with only positive results. This feature opens the realm of possibilities for appropriate tasks to offload to a virtual assistant.

Furthermore, since your tasks are no longer limited to one capable person, scaling becomes automatic and painless. Communicating exclusively through e-mail means that you can assign tasks whenever and wherever you are. My favorite is to do a complete "brain dump" at the end of the day before bed. I'll often shoot off ten or twelve tasks that would otherwise bug me for hours and affect my sleep. By utilizing this part of my external brain, as far as I'm concerned, the task is done the second I send the request. I can rest easy. What's more, this process creates a searchable record of all your tasks. Zirtual has a dashboard that provides an overview of all your requests as well as the status, communications, and exchanged files for each specific task.

What to Outsource to a Virtual Assistant

There is a great list of common requests on Zirtual, and my e-book on virtual assistants lists more than a hundred tasks you can have a VA perform. I'm going to examine several sample tasks and show you how to achieve them with your new setup. If no explanation is given, it simply means the request requires no additional input because the VA can handle it. I hope I'll provide enough of a framework so that you can attack your specific tasks that aren't covered here.

STRAIGHT REQUESTS WITH NO ADDITIONAL TOOLS NEEDED:

- Web or phone research

- Making dinner or travel reservations

- Following up with a client by phone

- Proofreading

- Updating a document, spreadsheet, or PowerPoint presentation

- Cold-calling (provide a script)

- Creating an Excel spreadsheet from provided or found data set

- Product comparison

- Content summaries

- Grocery delivery orders

- Donating items to charity and arranging pickup

- Adding your website or business information to search directories

- Document formatting or conversion

- Customer service

- Fact-checking

- Travel research

- Finding the nearest store with an item in stock

TASKS THAT NEED ADDITIONAL TOOLS:

- Schedule meetings. Use ScheduleOnce (www.scheduleonce.com) to share your schedule with the VA and allow him/her to make appointments for you. Your schedule link should be in your e-mail signature.

- Check, transcribe, and respond to voice mails. Use Google Voice (www.google.com/voice) to get voice mails by e-mail and simply forward them to the assistant.

- Transcribe audio or take dictations. Use your favorite voice-recording program (I like Recordium—www.recordiumapp.com) to send the VA an audio file for transcription. It could be a short blog post or letter, or just an idea you want to get out of your head.

- Mail letters. Using PostalMethods (www.postalmethods.com), remote assistants can send PDFs through postal mail, to individuals or entire mailing lists.

- Share passwords securely. Use LastPass (www.lastpass.com).

- Perform complex and/or repetitive tasks. Google's Canned Responses allows you to create template e-mails in Gmail so you can write something down step by step and save it as a template. That way, it's just one click away the next time you need it done. For repetitive tasks, you can use Boomerang (www.boomerang.com) to send recurring messages, which may be one of your Canned Responses. An example would be to have an assistant log in to a site (with details provided in the template), check stats, and give you a report each week.

- Real-world physical tasks. Use TaskRabbit (www.taskrabbit.com) for general stuff and RedBeacon (www.redbeacon.com) for home services.

- Bookkeeping. Combine weekly check-ins with the virtual bookkeeping services of Bench (www.bench.co).

- Lead generation or getting new prospects for your business. Using Canned Responses, Boomerang recurring messages, and a script, VAs can do systematic, weekly lead-generation work.

- Blog content moderation. Use Canned Responses to provide log-in information and Boomerang to have it done on a regular schedule.

- Craigslist or eBay postings. Use Canned Responses to provide log-in information and a template; you just provide specifics and photos.

- Expense reporting. Use Canned Responses and a shared Google Docs spreadsheet to send a photo of a receipt and have it parsed and entered into an expense report.

- Sort and process postal mail. Use Virtual Post Mail (www.virtualpostmail .com) to receive physical mail virtually.

- Incoming check management and deposits. Using Virtual Post Mail, checks can be reconciled and deposits can be made by mail.

- Research interesting blog and news items. Star an item you find interest-ing in feedly or favorite a tweet and use IFTTT to automatically archive and share it for further research.

TASKS THAT SHOULD BE AUTOMATED:

- Wake-up calls. WakerUpper (www.wakerupper.com)

- Waiting on hold. Fast Customer (www.fastcustomer.com) or Lucy Phone (www.lucyphone.com)

- Adding business cards to your address book. CardMunch (www.cardmunch.com)

- Making dinner reservations. OpenTable (www.opentable.com)

- Follow up by e-mail. FollowUp.cc (www.followup.cc)

- Sending thank-you notes. Postable (www.postable.com)

- Meal delivery. Seamless (www.seamless.com) or Delivery (www.delivery.com)

- Text messages/phone reminders/escape calls. IFTTT (www.IFTTT.com)

- Ordering a car service. Uber (www.Uber.com) or GroundLink (www.groundlink.com)

Obviously, there are plenty of tasks that require more than twenty minutes, such as extensive research projects, social media management, ghostwriting, financial modeling, travel planning, and graphic or web design work. For these kinds of projects, it's almost always better to hire a project-based specialist on Elance. A specialist will have the best talent for the job and will be the most cost effective.

OUTSOURCING YOUR OUTSOURCING

Once you know how to work with a virtual assistant, the pinnacle of achievement in outsourcing is to outsource not just the tasks themselves, but also the process of outsourcing them. Even better, automate the process of assigning tasks to your assistants!

I've achieved this with IFTTT. It started with a simple assignment to my Fancy Hands virtual assistant: "Find out how to automatically submit new blog posts to StumbleUpon."

It's pretty unusual to stump a Fancy Hands assistant, but the response I got back was, "There is no current method for automatically submitting blog posts to StumbleUpon."

I held my breath for the briefest of moments. Then my mouth pulled into a smile. I like challenges like this. I didn't realize this would open a completely new realm of outsourcing for me.

It's one thing to use an on-demand virtual assistant for standard tasks, but recurring tasks are tricky, since your tasks are assigned to different assistants each time. Initially, I got around this by creating a reminder from Re:snooze with the task instructions. You can have this message sent to you at a certain interval—when it arrives, simply forward it to the assistant.

I thought that was a pretty slick solution, but it still required a moment of my involvement. The issue with Re:snooze is that it's not trigger-based, only interval-based. So, the task might read, "Add new posts from the past week," but it couldn't read, "Add the post that *just* went up."

Another approach I tried was to create a forwarding filter through Gmail. The problem was, the resulting e-mail didn't originate from my own e-mail address. Because of that, most virtual assistant routing services wouldn't recognize it—they rejected the task.

This time, I approached the task backward and on a very basic level. How could I assign a task to my virtual assistant without having to initiate the request at all? I was seeking the holy grail of outsourcing, the perpetual motion machine of the outsourcing world: I wanted to outsource my outsourcing.

Since mind control of Gmail doesn't exist·and wouldn't be a realistic solution anyway (why use my mind for that?), I started to scratch my head. I remembered that IFTTT has a Gmail channel, which I'd never used before. You can create triggers based on searches or starring an item, but you can also send an e-mail.

But wait, does this sent e-mail originate from your own e-mail address? *Yes, it does!!!*

I was so excited, I could hardly contain myself. That's when I created the first

IFTTT recipe, which has resulted in thirty-two outstanding and amazing auto-mated actions that I never have to think about again. It couldn't have been more simple: if a new post (based on the RSS feed for my blog) is created, then send a Gmail e-mail message to request@fhands.com with, "Visit this [feed URL] and submit this newly published post to StumbleUpon."

IFTTT gives you several options for automatically propagating information, so "[feed URL]" is replaced with the most recent post address. That's all there is to it. According to the 80/20 Rule, I should be focusing only on the things that only I can do, like creating original content for the blog. Everything else should be handled by someone else if at all possible.

IFTTT has about fifty channels at this point, most of which can cause an e-mail to be sent to your virtual assistant. I set up a trigger so that every Fri-day morning, my assistant receives an e-mail telling him/her to create my "In-teresting Things of the Week" post, based on my Delicious links from the past seven days.

You may ask, why not just give your assistant one instruction: "Create the post every Friday"? For one thing, if you don't have a dedicated assistant, then you can't do that. But even if you do have a dedicated assistant, what hap-pens when that person gets sick or takes a new job? Doing things my way makes you future-proof, bombproof, and idiot-proof.

Think how much fun you can have with this! How about every time you take an Instagram picture of a cool product and tag it with the word "#buythis," your assistant gets an e-mail instructing him or her to find it at the best price and order it? Maybe on rainy days you decide to indulge in an Uber car instead of walking to the train. So you set an IFTTT recipe that checks the weather and, if rain is predicted, it sends an e-mail to your virtual assistant asking him or her to order you a car to take you to work. You could get creative and say that if you check in on Foursquare at a place categorized as an airport, your assistant gets an e-mail instructing him/her to contact family and work colleagues to let them know you've arrived safely.

The more you can make things happen based on the things you are already doing, the less stressed and more productive you'll be.

FUNDAMENTAL 3

Customization

W e live in a society that offers options for customization of just about everything imaginable. Food, clothes, vehicles, and even a box of LEGOs can be designed and manufactured specifically for you. This is not a narcissistic pursuit—there is tangible value in getting exactly what you want and leaving out what you don't.

We're fortunate to live in a world where we have great access to thousands of products at cheap prices, all readily available. When a product is created to work for everybody, however, there's a good chance it won't be exactly right for you. If a problem presents itself to you, a solution may or may not exist. If it doesn't, creating it may be easier than you think.

The basic principles behind customization are to save time, save money, and simply provide a better solution. I'd like to give you three examples from my life that exemplify these three principles well.

The first example is Vitamins on Demand. Vitamins on Demand provides custom vitamin packs in a little cardboard folder for each week. It's designed to let you break off a pack for each day, several days, or even the whole week at a time. This makes traveling a breeze and allows you to grab all your vitamins as you run out the door.

Being health conscious is an important part of the Less Doing lifestyle. As we eliminate work tasks from our lives, we naturally focus on more important things, one of which is physical well-being.

I take six supplements on a daily basis: krill oil, iron, vitamin B Complex, probiotics, ginger, and cat's claw (an Amazonian plant known for its anti-inflammatory benefits). I normally got each of these from different sources, and they all had different doses. This meant that I would run out of them at different times, and I'd usually forget to order refills in time. I sent Vitamins on Demand one e-mail, describing exactly what results I wanted. Within a few hours I had a price (about half what I normally pay) and a full nutritional information sheet. I also set up an auto shipment plan so I never have to think about it again.

As an added bonus, Vitamins on Demand has an entrepreneurial component. If you come up with an amazing combo, they will print labels for you and suddenly you have a new business! Many customization sites offer you an immediate platform to sell your creations.

The second great act of customization in my life comes from Indochino, a custom suit company. Indochino walks you through a thorough ten-minute measuring process, complete with video examples. They save your profile in their system. Then, they present you with several dozen suits in different styles, from tuxedos to three-piece banker suits. The suits start at around two hundred and fifty dollars. This is an excellent price for a custom suit, and if the measurements are off, they'll give you a seventy-five-dollar credit to go to a tailor and get it fixed. You can specify pocket styles, lining colors, and even have your name monogrammed on the inside of the jacket. When the seasons change and you decide it's time for something new, you simply pick the style you like, knowing that it will be a perfect fit, every time.

The last example of customization I'll give you is Ponoko. Ponoko is an interesting community of "makers" and on-demand 3D printing services. Ponoko can help turn an idea into a product—if, for example, you have a design for a better coffee cup or a really cool desk chair.

How does this contribute to Less Doing? Let's say you have a desk that is really perfect for your big desktop computer and monitor. Times are changing and you want to upgrade to a Mac mini and mount that huge studio display on the wall. Wouldn't it be nice to have a clutter-free desk for all the pen holders, drink rests, and cable management slots you want?

If you have some design skills, you could model it yourself, but that would take too much time. That's where Ponoko comes in. You can post your request, and someone will bid to design it for you. When the design is complete, you can have it laser cut or three-dimensionally printed in metal, wood, or even glass. They can also include electronic components like accelerometers and GPS. You can also use the site to get completely unique gifts for people, saving you the time and wasted effort of searching for the "perfect gift" that doesn't exist. (Other similar sites include Shapeways and Kraftwurx.)

WHERE TO START

There are many companies devoted to creating custom products. Sometimes, a quick Internet search may find you a company that will make exactly what you want. Other times, you may need an expert to create it for you.

If what you need is less tangible, like software or travel planning, you can find someone to do it for you on Elance. From my perspective, Elance is the number-one outsourcing marketplace in the world—much better than Guru and Odesk. It's free to post the job you want done. Once you post the project, people from around the world bid on it. There's an escrow system, and you can check the contractor's feedback before you hire anyone. Elance has experts in many different fields, from software development and graphic design to travel planning, legal advice, and private investigation. It's a great way to get the job done.

Another favorite outsourcing website is www.fiverr.com. Fiverr is a site where people will do gigs for five dollars, ranging from the extremely bizarre to the very useful. On the bizarre side, there's a guy in New York City who, for five dollars, will call anybody you want and wish them happy birthday . . . as Christopher Walken. He's making fifteen hundred dollars a month doing this.

There's also an older gentleman who will do a fake skydiving video holding a sign with your website written on it for five dollars—weird stuff.

But there's also really useful stuff, like "I will tweet your message to my 240,000 Twitter followers in the next twenty-four hours for five dollars." Or "I will submit your site to 1,250 search engine directories for five dollars."

Or "I will review your website and give you ten tips for improving your search engine optimization for five dollars." They all have feedback, and there's some really good stuff.

A few years ago, when I bought my Mac mini, I put these services together to create a custom bracket to mount it on the wall. I can't draw, but I was able to make a terrible drawing of what I wanted. Then I paid someone five dollars on Fiverr to turn the drawing into a 3D model. Then I sent the 3D model to www.shapeways.com. Shapeways charges by the amount of material, so for forty-three dollars, I was able to get a 3D printed prototype of my 3D model. A week later, it came in the mail, and I had the perfect bracket to hang my Mac mini on the wall.

On top of that, if you use Shapeways, you also get access to their e-commerce platform. I ended up selling six of these brackets for sixty-five dollars apiece. So, with about an hour of my time and an initial cost of forty-eight dollars, I was able to create a custom-made one-off product that was exactly suited to my needs, and make almost four hundred dollars selling that product to other people. If a solution doesn't already exist, you can probably create one a lot more easily than you might think.

Occasionally, the process of customization can be more trouble than it's worth. When it comes to the things that we interact with on a constant basis, however, there is almost always a way to do it more efficiently. If your first attempt at customization is unsuccessful, it's important not to become discouraged. To paraphrase Thomas Edison, you simply found a way not to do what you were trying to accomplish. Give it another shot.

If you're using a product or service and wonder if there is a better way, odds are that you can create one with very little effort. In doing so, you'll be one step closer to Less Doing.

Choose Your Own Workweek

Many people have heard of *The Four-Hour Workweek* by Tim Ferriss. The title is a bit facetious—Tim admittedly does more than four hours of work per week—but the idea is spot-on. You must define what a workweek is and then decide how much of your life you want it to occupy.

WHAT IS A WORKWEEK?

The concept of choosing your own workweek comes back to timing. This applies to people with 9-to-5 jobs as well as people with more flexible schedules. The idea is that some times are better than others for certain people to do certain things. By choosing your own workweek, you set up your schedule in order to match tasks to your best times for accomplishing them.

My workweek consists of the times when clients, vendors, and other business contacts can have a reasonable expectation of getting in touch with me and/or receiving some sort of work product. While your workweek will probably become the time that you get your work done, that is not what defines it.

My personal workweek was Tuesday through Thursday—now it's Tuesday and Wednesday, ten a.m. to four p.m. I actually started doing this back in college. In my senior year, I only took classes on Tuesdays and Thursdays. This meant that every weekend was a four-day weekend and I had a day of rest between the workdays. By batching classes into these two days, I was personally in my most efficient work mode.

As a member of the workforce, I originally had a five-day workweek like most people. Then I reduced it day by day, eventually settling at my current schedule.

It's not that I only work two days a week. I'm working all the time, and I love what I do. I sometimes work seven days a week. I work late at night, any time— if what I'm doing is interesting, it doesn't matter. My workweek is also a guideline: if something comes up on a Friday, I'm not going to ignore it, but I make sure 95 percent of all the things that I do for work that involve other people fall on Tuesdays and Wednesdays.

This doesn't mean that every weekend *might* be a five-day weekend. Every weekend *is* a five-day weekend. The logic behind this is simple. We can over-generalize and say that most inefficiencies come from other people in your life, rather than your internal issues. A supplier might be late, a client might have trouble making up his mind, or an electric company refuses to join the twenty-first century by offering electronic billing. By shortening the window in which clients can interact with you, you automatically force batching on their part as well as yours. Essentially, you force everyone to work more efficiently.

I chose the middle of the week because it works best with my schedule. I like to go to my farm in the country on the weekend and not have to worry about Friday-night or Monday-morning traffic. It also means I can avoid the drowsi-ness of everyone's Monday recovery from the weekend, as well as their lack of attention on Fridays as they count down the minutes until their weekend.

On Tuesday and Wednesday, I know I'll have hectic days, but this form of batching fuels me to power through with motivation and efficiency. At the end of each day, the feeling of accomplishment is busting out of me.

On top of that, gaining control over your schedule has a profound psy-chological effect. The number-one complaint I hear is that people are over-whelmed by their e-mail, all the tasks they have to do, all the meetings they have to attend, and their work in general. Taking a little control over your work-week can make a big difference.

The structure that makes the most sense for your workweek will depend on your work and industry. The key is experimentation.

HOW TO MAKE IT HAPPEN

You can make this work using two key plug-ins. The first is ScheduleOnce, a scheduling application that gives you a free public scheduling interface and appointment page. If you went to my ScheduleOnce page, you would see my availability for the week. You could request a meeting with me, and if I agree, it gets added to each of our calendars.

Without a system like this, it takes an average of seven e-mails to set up a meeting. This changes it to one, which saves time in itself. The link to my schedule is in my e-mail signature, and if someone wants to meet with me, I can say, "Here's my schedule. Pick any time that works for you."

What they don't realize is that when they go to that page, they only see Tuesday and Wednesday availability. As far as they know, I'm just really busy on Monday, Thursday, and Friday.

When prospective clients try this, they love it. They want to sign up right away to work with me. I'm giving them the freedom to pick any time they want, so things go much more smoothly. It also means you don't have to worry about saying no to people or fitting them into the right times. For me, I know that Tuesday and Wednesday are going to be hectic, but it also means that if those two days get filled up, the person simply schedules for next week instead of having the awkward conversation where people try to get you to work them into your schedule this week. This way, it's not just, "I don't want to meet with you this week"—they can see that you're not available, so they move on to a time when you are.

The second key plug-in is called Right InBox, and it works with Gmail. It does four things: delays the sending of an e-mail, tracks the opening of an e-mail, tracks if any of the links in an e-mail get clicked, and reminds you to follow up. The reminder feature duplicates FollowUp.cc, but the others are very useful.

For example, when I get an e-mail on Friday afternoon, I might want to deal with it immediately and get it out of my head. But we've all sent an e-mail at four p.m. on Friday and received a reply at 4:59 that ruins our weekend because we can't really do anything about it until Monday, but there it is in the inbox. Instead of doing that to somebody, I like to write those e-mails and send them out Friday afternoon but not have them delivered until Monday morning.

That way, it's off my plate and I don't have to think about it again, but it arrives on Monday, when the recipient is better prepared to deal with it.

For my workweek of Tuesday and Wednesday, I may write the e-mail on Wednesday but not have it sent out until Tuesday morning, when I'll be back in work mode and ready to respond. That's a little extreme, but it allows you a lot of flexibility, and sometimes it makes sense. If you can limit communication with others to your workdays, you can channel people into learning the best times to deal with you: during *your* workweek.

Of course, there will be times when someone is only able to meet outside of your workweek. There's nothing wrong with making exceptions in these circumstances because it is your decision. One meeting in a whole day won't hurt too much.

Remember, your workweek is not the time when you do your work, it's the time during which business contacts can interact with you. You can limit this to as much or as little time as works best for you.

FUNDAMENTAL 5

Stop Running Errands

. . . .

I don't want you to run errands, ever ever ever again. They're not efficient, and there's no way to make them efficient. They're a waste of your time.

The number-one service I recommend to eliminate errands is Amazon Subscribe and Save. It allows you to subscribe to nonperishable items that Amazon sells: dog food, toilet paper, toothpaste, and other things like that. You can set what you want and how much—for example, three tubes of toothpaste every two months. You can cancel any delivery at any time, and you can get an extra delivery at any time, so it's hardly even a subscription, and you immediately get a 5 to 15 percent discount for buying this way. Most important, once you set it up, you don't have to think about it anymore.

Using Subscribe and Save is definitely cheaper, and it's simpler than buying stuff in person. Even if you go to Costco, it's a lot of stuff to carry, and there's a good chance you'll forget something or buy something you don't need. With Subscribe and Save, Amazon basically becomes your digital pantry. I've already saved thousands of hours using this service. Over the last three years, my wife and I have not had to shop for things like toilet paper, dish detergent, paper towels, soap, razors, deodorant, baby food, diapers, dog food—the list goes on. It's set it and forget it: I set it up, and now I don't have to worry about it anymore.

If you don't live in a building with a doorman or you have a hard time receiving packages, they've figured this out, too. They have a service called Amazon Lockers. There are about fifty locations throughout New York City, which are set up like bus station lockers, where you can have your package delivered and you get a message telling you it's there and ready for you.

Subscribe and Save is great for products with timing issues associated with them. For example, my wife and I use Brita filters. Every two months, we get a shipment of Brita filters. Now, instead of running out of filters, ordering more, waiting for them to come, and installing the new ones, I just get the shipment, know it's time to change the filters, and put the new ones in. It's out of my head. Similarly, every six months, we need to change the batteries in the smoke detectors, so every six months, we get a shipment of 9-volt batteries. When the batteries come, I change them. I never have to think about it or remember, and I never have a smoke detector beeping in the middle of the night. Peace of mind, time saved, money saved—works for me!

For errands that you can't eliminate or automate, it's time to outsource. You can get someone to do these real-world, in-person tasks for you. One such service is called TaskRabbit. It's a lot like Elance but for real-world tasks.

You can use the TaskRabbit iPhone app to enter a request by voice or text. You tell them what you need and when you need it, and a TaskRabbit provider will complete the task for you. It's a competitive market among the helpers, so you'll get fast responses and competitive rates. TaskRabbit can handle tasks like dropping off donations for charity, buying groceries, taking your car to the shop, hanging a shelf in your apartment, fixing your computer, and doing your holiday shopping. The site will also offer suggestions, free of charge.

All TaskRabbit service providers go through a background check, and it's not just for basic errands. They also have specialists, such as personal chefs and masseuses.

Here's an example to give you a better idea of what this type of service can do for you. I have a nephew in Los Angeles, and three months ago, it was his second birthday. His mom told us he wanted a particular slide from IKEA. From New York City, I contracted someone through TaskRabbit. I had this person go to IKEA in Long Beach, get the slide, take it to my nephew's house, and put it together. He even sang happy birthday to my nephew—and all for forty-seven dollars!

It's not that my time is better than their time. It's about batching. The people who do this stuff do it all the time. It's a really incredible thing, and it's time better spent. The idea is to get down to the 5 percent of tasks that only you can do, and only do those things. Then you can work on those things and maximize your efficiency and your skill set.

ARE YOU READY?

There you have it. You've got nothing to lose and everything to gain by getting other people to run your errands and handle your simple tasks. Rid yourself of the minutiae and start focusing on the things that make you happy.

FUNDAMENTAL 6

Finances

. . . .

The Less Doing lifestyle is about efficiency, and we believe this efficiency should translate to financial savings, too. It's not enough to simply manage your finances. We want you be a financial sushi chef, cutting out all the fat and leaving nothing but the tastiest bits. (Now I'm thinking about sushi. . . .)

To accomplish these goals, you need a clear picture of where your money is and where it's going. To start, you should be signed up for electronic statements with all of your banks so you don't get the paper; everything stays organized online.

WHERE'S MY MONEY AND WHERE AM I SPENDING IT?

Typically, a person might have a checking and savings account at a bank, a debit card, a credit card, and maybe some kind of 401(k) or investment portfolio.

If you have a business (or several), you know the accounts you have can multiply and quickly become unmanageable. That's where Mint.com comes in. You supply the site with the log-in details for your various banking sites. You input personal accounts, credits cards, business accounts, auto loans, and stock portfolios. If you want something that's strictly for business, you should use InDinero, which adds access for an accountant. It automatically pulls in all your information every day, categorizing transactions and giving you a very nice overview of your financial health. Mint will e-mail you when an account has a low balance or when a particularly large deposit clears. This is very convenient if you want to make sure that a paycheck made it into your account.

Once everything is in and the system starts analyzing, you can discover things about yourself. Mint can also set budgets based on past spending, and alert you when you exceed those levels. So if you notice that you're spending a lot of money on restaurants this month, it might be time to start cooking at home. The site will also show you credit card and checking account offers and exactly how much money they will save you in the long run.

Mint gives you a nice dashboard for oversight of your finances. It's easy to lose sight of how we're doing things and how we're spending time and resources. Using a site like Mint can pull you back.

To go beyond Mint and get really serious about analytics, you need to check out OneReceipt. This service automatically pulls in all of your e-receipts from your e-mail. It also lets you add paper receipts by snapping a picture and e-mailing it to them. At the end of each month, it generates a personal expense report and shows you how much you spent at Amazon, iTunes, the grocery store, the gas station—wherever you spend money. (Is it bad that 28 percent of my monthly income goes to Amazon?)

OneReceipt also has a plug-in for Firefox and Chrome that works with American Express, Citibank, Bank of America, and Mint. If you hover over a transaction, the receipt will pop up, so you know what you bought in each transaction (especially handy if you have twenty Amazon transactions in the same month). If you return something, you know when the money gets credited back to your account.

Similarly, another service called Slice can scan all your e-mail receipts and create a dashboard showing all your deliveries, so you know when something is coming and how much money you spent where.

In addition to monitoring online purchases, you can monitor your credit cards using a service called BillGuard. This service watches all of your credit card transactions and flags any transactions that it finds suspicious: things like double fees and international transactions. Each month, you get a report showing the flagged transactions. For each transaction, you can see more information about the company, and there's a button for disputing the charge if you want to. It is all very quick and easy, and keeps you from having to pore through pages of banking transactions.

This is especially useful for me, because my one vice is buying stuff from infomercials. I don't know why, but if it's on at three o'clock in the morning, I own it. The problem is, those transactions often come up as "FSR Industries Unlimited International, Inc.," and you have no idea what that is, especially when you have multiple similar transactions. In BillGuard, you can click one button, and it will find out for you.

Another great set-it-and-forget-it application is FileThis.com. It automatically pulls e-statements from utility companies, cell phone providers, credit card companies, and other bills each month. It gathers these statements in PDF form and puts them in Evernote. Suddenly, it's all searchable!

I manage rental properties, so I have access to twelve different business bank accounts. Finding something manually was a big problem, but now I can search in Evernote and get directly to the right paper statement. In addition, it files the statements for each account into its own notebook, and you can share notebooks, so I can share statements with my assistant and accountant automatically without having to give them secure access to my bank accounts.

SAVE SOME DOUGH

Once you know where your money is going, you can start optimizing. I'm a big fan of a site called BillShrink. You provide a few details about your driving habits, checking account, cell phone usage (which can be pulled from your provider's site), and television service. BillShrink uses that information to give you very real, very personal options for saving money. Based on your data, the site shows alternative options for these services and how much money they could save you over the next two years. After about ten minutes with BillShrink, I realized that I could save about fourteen thousand dollars over the next two years. The site e-mails you as new deals become available.

The process of being efficient is one of constant evolution and adaptation, and it's very easy to get comfortable with your current credit card or checking account. BillShrink helps you pinpoint the little bit of effort necessary to save a sizable amount of money by switching providers.

DEBIT EXCLUSIVITY

Another option for people who want to simplify as much as possible, especially those who travel frequently, is to eschew credit cards and only use debit cards.

Nowadays, debit or check cards offer many of the same benefits as credit cards in terms of loyalty rewards and purchase protection. A debit-only solution means you don't get a credit card bill, and you never have to worry about paying interest or late fees, or actually going into debt. It's simple: if you don't have the money in your account, you can't spend it. American Express credit cards are not accepted in many parts of the world and often not for small purchases, so debit cards are more convenient in that way, too.

To get a handle on your finances, you need to analyze your spending to determine the best way to cut the excess fat. Start with an organization system, simplify, and get a little help from deal recommendation sites.

FUNDAMENTAL 7

Organization

I t should go without saying that organization is paramount to efficiency.

Organization comes in many forms, from mental checklists to e-mail processes to designing the layout of your physical space. All forms are important, depending on the task at hand. Many people find it difficult to get or stay organized, but we have a method that is simple to execute and requires only a modicum of discipline. It's all about setting limits.

WHAT LIMITS?

Upper limits and lower limits each have a place and can be useful in their own right. You need to set and abide by a reasonable limit for yourself in any task you complete.

Accountants would view this as a "FIFO" system, or "First In, First Out." The most concrete example I can give is my electronics stash. I used to have a closet completely dedicated to electronic gear. There was a shelf for audio cables, a shelf for network cables, an area with all kinds of dead technology like a wristwatch walkie-talkie (What? I was a budding secret agent . . .), and a whole mess of other stuff. I didn't know where anything was, so on the rare occasion when I needed a network patch cable, I would make a bigger mess just trying to find it.

After selling most of the stuff on eBay and recycling the rest, I now have a single egg crate for electronics. It holds a couple of cables, an old webcam, and some other miscellaneous items. The box is my absolute, no-questions-asked limit for storing electronic gear. The box is always filled, so whenever something new comes along that I want to put in the box, I have to get rid of something already in there. This forces me to make a decision about whether or not I really need that new thing, or if it's more important than something at the bottom of the box that I haven't seen in months.

The other day, I bought a new cordless phone for our house, and it came with a new telephone cord. I took a look at the bottom of the box, and there were a couple in there already, so the new one definitely was not a keeper. It's very satisfying to have that one small box in the closet instead of using the entire closet.

WHAT ABOUT EVERYTHING ELSE?

You name it! Whether it's e-mail, grocery shopping, time on Facebook, or your workweek, you can set a limit on anything. You should never have more than fifty e-mails in your inbox, you don't need eight boxes of cereal (unless you're a house mom at a large fraternity), you shouldn't spend more than a few minutes per hour on Facebook, and your workweek should never, ever be seven days long. Everything can and should have a limit, even leisure time (which should have a lower limit).

Upper limits are obvious, but many people miss the other side of the coin: the minimum limits to the things we do. These apply very well to travel (I want to take one trip per month), fitness (I will run thirty miles per week), nutrition (I will cook at home three times per week), and so on. Limits can refer to times or amounts, whatever makes the most sense.

The key is picking a realistic limit and sticking to it. It's better to be conservative and hit your limits than to constantly fall short and cause yourself more frustration. For instance, a cigar box for my electronics would have been too ambitious.

To give an example, I have a limit of ten e-mails in my inbox. I refuse to have more than that many in there, ever. Right now I have six.

I can keep the e-mail within that limit because I have filters set up, I have a virtual assistant, I have autoresponders—I've reduced the amount of e-mail I get to the point where I can keep up with it and never need to have more than ten messages in my inbox. If I found that I was consistently exceeding my limit, that would mean I needed to optimize the system more, or the VA needed to check in more frequently, or something else needed to change. Whatever that might be, it doesn't mean it can't be done.

When I switched from PC to Mac, I did so partly because I'd wanted to switch for a long time, but also partly because my PC died. I had a backup, but it was outdated. I lost some of my stuff. I decided I never wanted something like that to happen again, so I switched to keeping everything in the cloud. This was three years ago, when it wasn't as easy as it is now.

Since I keep everything in the cloud, I have only two programs on my computer: Dropbox and Chrome. I will not install anything else. That's my limit.

If there was something else I needed, I would either find another way to do the same thing on the web, or I would realize that I really didn't need that piece of software to do that task.

The beauty of that setup is that if my computer blew up right now, I could move to any other computer or iPad and be up and running in about three minutes. I actually decided to run my life entirely from my iPad, just to see if I could do it. After trying it for a week, I found that there were four or five things I couldn't do from the iPad, so I figured out how to do them. In some cases, it involved a new app that hadn't previously existed for iPad; in others, it involved sending things to my assistant, having her process them in some way, and having her send them back to me (or just do it for me). But I figured out how to do all of them from the iPad.

After that, I took it even further: could I do it from only the iPhone? My wife and I went to Los Angeles for a week, and I didn't take a laptop or an iPad, only my iPhone. I was able to successfully run my entire life and business—construction projects in Long Island, Less Doing projects, everything—all from my iPhone. In the whole week, there were only two hiccups, and I figured out how to get around both of them from the road.

Realistically, I'm not going to be running my business on a daily basis with only an iPhone, but it's great to know I can if I need to. That means the iPad is about ten times more efficient and the computer is about a hundred times more efficient, as I'm benefitting from a larger screen and more processing power.

To streamline your life and help yourself get organized, always set reasonable limits for the things you do. If you find yourself running up against those limits, it usually means something else must go.

FUNDAMENTAL 8

Batching

Batching is the flip side of what we discussed in the fourth Fundamental, Choose Your Own Workweek: we're batching similar tasks together to gain efficiency. Batching is all about "getting in the zone" and minimizing transition time. Instead of constantly getting interrupted and switching focus, you let similar tasks accumulate and deal with them all at once.

For example, some people decide they only do e-mail in the first ten minutes of any given hour. They let messages build up over the hour, then dispatch them all at once. This way, they avoid the gearshift mentality of changing tasks every time an e-mail comes in.

To give another example, my wife and I cook dinner for the week on Sundays. It allows us to spend a few hours enjoying cooking, and then we either freeze the food or put it in the fridge in portions for the week.

I also deal with my paperwork for the week all at once on Friday morning, rather than throughout the week as bills come in. For any errands that can't be outsourced, never do just one. Figure out what else you need to buy and then think about the most efficient way to do it. For example, if you need to stop by the drugstore, try to do it on your commute back from work.

As you think about what tasks you could do in batches, remember that it's even better to eliminate those tasks altogether if you can. Since many small nuisance tasks involve processing paper in one way or another, I put together some tools that can help you reduce the flow of paper in your life. In some cases, eliminating the paper means you can stop doing these tasks altogether.

THIRTEEN TECH TOOLS FOR A PAPER-FREE LIFE

1. LifeLock: www.lifelock.com

LifeLock is a service that helps prevent identity theft by automatically removing your name from every mailing list you don't want to be a part of. The service renews monthly to ensure you are permanently removed from lists and not placed on new ones. Within three months of signing up for LifeLock, I had reduced my paper mail intake by about 70 percent.

2. Catalog Choice: www.catalogchoice.org

Catalog Choice is a nonprofit that works with companies to make sure catalogs get sent to people who want them and not to you. This free service lets you search through a huge database and remove your name from any listing.

3. Square Reader: www.squareup.com

The Square Reader app allows you to accept credit card payments from your iPhone at low rates and with no monthly fees. Payments are approved instantly, and both you and the buyer get copies of the receipt via e-mail. You also don't need to carry the physical card reader with you. You can enter the card number manually at a slightly higher percent charge.

4. HelloFax: www.hellofax.com

HelloFax gives you a local fax number that delivers to your e-mail inbox. You can seamlessly fill in forms, sign documents, request signatures from others, and fax the documents back. It's been about three years since I've held a faxed piece of paper in my hands.

5. SignNow: www.signnow.com

With SignNow, you can easily forward a document from anywhere, including your iPhone. In a few minutes you'll receive an e-mail that lets you sign anywhere, fill in fields, and send it to someone else for a signature. It's similar to HelloFax except it's free, doesn't have the fax element, and works well on mobile.

6. Doxie: www.getdoxie.com

Doxie is a small, efficient scanner that will digitize your documents directly into cloud services like Dropbox and Google Docs. There will soon be a version that doesn't require a computer, so you can scan anywhere and then sync up when you return.

7. PostalMethods: www.postalmethods.com

If you still need to send physical mail, PostalMethods lets you upload a document with its web interface or via e-mail. The company will print it out, put it in an envelope, stamp it, and mail it. Never lick a stamp again.

8. Virtual Post Mail: www.virtualpostmail.com

For any remaining mail, consider a virtual mailbox. Virtual Post Mail will give you a post office box and display any received mail in an organized web portal. You can then decide if you want to have Virtual Post Mail open and scan the contents, recycle it, or forward it to any address in the world. You can also set it up to automatically perform a selected action for a given sender. That way, you can download and forward images as PDF files, check your mail on the beach in Thailand, or let a virtual assistant handle it for you. Virtual Post Mail also has a check-depositing feature. This is great, especially if you manage rental properties or deal with a lot of checks. You can have them sent directly to Virtual Post Mail, and for a dollar per check, they will be deposited at the bank for you.

9. CardMunch: www.cardmunch.com

CardMunch is an app that turns a picture of a business card into a tran-scribed piece of information sent to your phone. The scanned card is added to the contact in your address book, making it their picture. LinkedIn owns this free app, so the person added to your contacts is also one click away from a connection request.

10. CamScanner: www.camscanner.net

For bigger documents, CamScanner is an application that lets you use your phone as a scanner. When you take a picture of the document, it finds the edges, adjusts perspective, and enhances text and images. Then you have a PDF you can e-mail or upload to one of your cloud services.

11. ScanDigital: www.scandigital.com

ScanDigital is great for those old boxes of photos fading away in your basement. Send all of your old media—photos, VHS tapes, and even slides. ScanDigital will scan and digitize everything for you. Now you can really enjoy those photos by carrying them on your mobile device to share with friends and family. For scanning entire books like textbooks or manu-scripts, you can use 1DollarScan (www.1dollarscan.com); they will scan a hundred pages for just a dollar.

12. Shoeboxed: www.shoeboxed.com

Shoeboxed is great for outsourcing paperwork. The service mainly cata-logs receipts, but you can also send any other paper product. It also pro-vides pre-addressed and stamped envelopes. Mobile apps are available to capture receipts and business cards on the go. All pertinent informa-tion is organized, so if you need to do expense reports or taxes, your life will be so much easier. You can also send in reams of paperwork to clear out for a fresh start. Everything is scanned and organized for you in an online portfolio.

13. TaskRabbit: www.taskrabbit.com

For the odd paper-based tasks that will inevitably happen every once in a while, you need to get a person involved. I use TaskRabbit to turn my handwritten notes into something more useful. (These are few and far between, thanks to Evernote, of course.)

The list goes on. It will be different for every person, but stop and think about how you spend your time and what tasks you find yourself repeating frequently. If you can't eliminate them, look at how they could be combined for greater efficiency.

WARNING!

Although batching can be a powerful time-saver, be careful not to take it too far. If you wait too long to do something, batching can easily overwhelm you. You need to set a schedule or threshold for batching and stick to it.

For instance, I try to do all of my laundry every Sunday. Laundry once a week is perfect timing. By the end of the week, my laundry baskets (whites, cold, and hot) are close to full. It takes me a couple of hours at home to throw in three loads of laundry and iron a few things. During the downtime, I'll do other batched tasks, such as cook for the week.

Once in a while, I will miss a Sunday. That's why I have plenty of underwear. The next Sunday is a bit unpleasant because I have to stay home for a while to do my laundry, but it's manageable.

Miss that second Sunday though, and the world feels like it's ending. The amount of laundry becomes unmanageable, and I often get stuck in a cycle of doing one load in the middle of the night when I realize I need dress socks for the next day.

Use batching wisely and think ahead to avoid that situation. Start to think in terms of batching everything. Every time you go to do a task, think, "Do I need to do this now, or could I wait until I have more similar tasks and do them all at once?" I believe most people can save five to ten hours a week by batching.

FUNDAMENTAL 9

Wellness

. . . .

Wellness is the foundation of everything else. As technologically efficient as I can make you, you're still a person.
If you're not sleeping enough or eating well, there's a limit to how
productive you can be.

Wellness means different things to different people, but to me, it comes
down to the amount of stress in my life and how I deal with that stress. Practi-
cally speaking, to attack stress we need to look at fitness and nutrition.

I couldn't possibly offer a panacea for everyone, because we are all so
individual.

I'm not here to offer a magical new diet plan or fitness regime. I'll simply
tell you a little about the experience I've had, framed in a context to show

you how to explore these options for yourself to find the best and most effective fit.

For an entire year while training for Ironman France, I spent more than twenty hours per week in a pool, on a bike, or running around the city. On days I had to do a bike ride that was longer than three hours, I'd get up at four a.m. and hop on the trainer in my office while I watched any and every random documentary on Netflix. It worked, because I achieved my goal of a sub-14-hour Ironman. But it wasn't particularly pleasant and I felt there had to be a better use of my time.

Unfortunately, if you are training for an Ironman, you have to put the time in. If for no other reason, you need to mentally train yourself for the agony of swimming 2.4 miles, biking 112 miles, and running a marathon. For everyone else, I'm here to tell you that you can get away with significantly less training.

Keep in mind that when I say "optimize," I'm talking about getting the maximum benefit for the least amount of energy and time. Remember the 80/20 Rule.

FITNESS

This applies to anyone who wants to lose weight, get healthier, and even train for an event of a distance up to and including a half-marathon or adventure race. If you are looking to qualify for the Boston Marathon or compete in an Ironman, the plan needs to change, but that is the exception, not the rule.

My three-part formula for perfect fitness is as follows:

- One part strength/skill. This could be your best five-rep back squat, clean-and-jerk, rock climbing, Parkour, or any other activity that involves some kind of skill.

- One part high-intensity interval training (HIIT). I recommend a CrossFit WOD (workout of the day), CrossFit Endurance WOD (involving swimming, biking, or running), Insanity, or any workout involving short bursts of maximal effort followed by active rest. You could even try a great free app called Sworkit.

- One part mobility. This may include yoga, a Mobility WOD, or just a good old stretching session.

You can do these over the course of three days (as I do), or you can combine them all into one super-session each week. Each segment should be around thirty minutes. You can certainly make them longer if you have the time and enjoy it, but it's not necessary. In fact, a recent study showed that those who worked out too much actually lost less weight than those who worked out a moderate amount. The hypothesis was that too much exercise increases appetite disproportionately with the number of calories burned through exercise.

To try this, get yourself a Fitbit and set appropriate goals. Here's what a typical week of fitness looks like for me:

- Tuesday, HIIT: swim 300m x 4 with a two-minute rest in between and try to hold the intervals within seven seconds of each other.

- Thursday, skill: 3 x 3 back squat (three reps, three times) and three reps max-weighted pull-up

- Sunday, Mobility: thirty-minute yoga session with the Pocket Yoga app on my iPhone

Like the rest of Less Doing, the goal here is to integrate things to make your life easier. Keep in mind that any fitness program will only work perfectly if your diet and sleep are under control. There is a three-way relationship among sleep, diet, and fitness, and there is usually a finite amount of energy you can allocate among them. This means that if you change one area, you have to change another to compensate. Sleep is the element that determines the amount of energy you have for the others.

SLEEP

Sleep is the cornerstone of a healthy lifestyle and the main determining factor of wellness. It's important to recognize that with sleep, it's really about quality, not quantity. There are many ways to affect your sleep—diet and exercise happen to be among the easiest to control.

As far as diet, eating too late at night will disrupt sleep quality, and eating too soon or too late after you wake up will affect your day. Eating good fats as part of a balanced diet helps your body to maintain balanced levels of hormones. Getting energy from fats instead of carbs means you'll have steadier, more focused fuel throughout the day. Proper exercise helps you burn unneeded energy, reset mentally, and reengage your body's resources.

When you don't sleep well, your body produces a hormone called ghrelin, which increases hunger and causes you to eat more. It also causes a dip in levels of leptin, a hormone that helps suppress appetite and regulates metabolism. Basically, if you don't sleep, be prepared for a major willpower battle that you will probably lose (avoid watching Travel Channel's *Man v. Food Nation*).

To improve sleep, I recommend two things. First, take some vitamin D with your breakfast and avoid any devices that emit blue light (iPads, TVs, LED lighting) at least one hour before bed, because these devices will disrupt your ability to produce melatonin. (You can wear blue-blocking glasses if you can't avoid these things and you don't mind looking like a serial killer.)

If you want to take things to the next level, you can always use a sleep tracker like SleepCycle and totally optimize your sleep patterns. You can also play around with very basic concepts of sleep timing.

The idea behind sleep timing is simple. The general sleep cycle is 1.5 hours, and you want at least three cycles per night. If you don't get enough, or if you wake up in the middle of a cycle, you won't feel well rested.

To find out when you need to go to bed, you can work backward from the time when you wake up, then add fifteen minutes to fall asleep. For example, if you need to get up at 5:30 a.m., then subtracting 1.5-hour intervals takes you to 4:00 a.m., 2:30 a.m., 1:00 a.m., 11:30 p.m. You also need to add fifteen minutes for falling asleep, so to get four complete cycles, you need to go to bed at 11:15 p.m. To get five cycles, you'd go to bed at 9:45 p.m.

If you're getting enough hours of sleep but waking up groggy, it could very well be because you're off by fifteen minutes and you're waking up at the wrong point in the cycle. That's an easy fix that can make a big difference.

NUTRITION

The third cornerstone of wellness is nutrition. Your diet should provide fuel for your life while protecting you from toxic elements in our environment. This means you should eat foods that are not processed, that you can identify (even sugar is better than aspartame), and, ideally, that you prepare yourself at home. With very few exceptions, anything you make at home should be healthier than what you get from a box or at a restaurant.

As I mentioned in the Introduction, my story with nutrition is a long and painful one as I struggled with Crohn's disease. After a great deal of self-tracking and self-experimentation, I was able to find a solution that worked for me, and maybe only me. Then I started experimenting with other diets and other people to get a broader sense of what was most effective. I wanted a healthy program that I could recommend to everyone—it needed to be easy to begin and maintain, and maybe even save money. In the end, it's all about knowing how food affects you, and maintaining balance.

It's actually a simpler concept than you might think. The first step is to track everything you eat for a week. You can use any tracking method, from pen and paper to an iPhone app such as Eater. You may be surprised at what you discover. In addition, write how you feel at the end of each day on a general good-mood or bad-mood metric.

Once you have a baseline, try to focus on consuming solely unprocessed foods, minimizing sugar, and increasing good fats like olive oil and avocado. Try not to have huge amounts of meat and no vegetables, or to have an all-carb day.

I don't recommend any one diet—everyone is different, so it's hard to recommend one thing that will work for everyone. But one thing does seem to be pretty universal here in America: we generally don't get enough good fats in our diet. In my opinion, the high-fat/low-carb diet is the healthiest and best diet.

I'm not talking about Atkins, because Atkins doesn't differentiate types of fat. I'm talking about good, healthy fat: avocados, olive oil, coconut oil, grass-fed butter, egg yolks from good eggs. I've tried a wide variety of diets, from 10,000 calories a day at 85 percent carbs, to my present 4,000 calories a day at 65 percent fat. With this diet, I'm not fat. My body fat percentage is the lowest it's ever been, and all of my blood markers (which I have checked regularly) are at their best.

Many people think fat is the enemy, but generally speaking, there are all sorts of problems with a low-fat diet. You can't absorb vitamins A, D, E, or K without fat, and fats are more satiating than protein and carbs. Perhaps most important, our brains are meant to run on fat.

Our brains are essentially like hybrid engines: they can run on ketones from fat, or on glucose from carbs. We produce more than enough glucose to run our brains on a daily basis, but we don't produce enough fat. Even if you're skinny, you have about 30,000 calories of available energy in your fat stores—enough to run two Ironmen. The key is getting your body to use that fat. I guarantee you will feel smarter, more focused, and more energetic if you can get your body on a fat burn instead of a carb burn.

Supplements

Supplements can act as the glue that binds together sleep, fitness, and nutrition. You can use supplements to improve and optimize each one and support a healthy lifestyle.

Generally, you should get essential elements from eating a good diet, but there are certain ones that are hard to get from food. Therefore, there are three supplements I recommend to people.

- Krill oil comes from tiny shrimp in the North Atlantic. It provides a variety of benefits, from reduced inflammation to lower cholesterol, and even better insulin response management. It's significantly more effective than fish oil.

- Probiotics are beneficial bacteria that keep your digestive system balanced, your immune response in order, and inflammation at bay.

- Vitamin D is an essential resource for your immune system, inflammation, and even sleep. Most people who work indoors, wear clothes, and don't get enough fat in their diets are vitamin D deficient.

The key to a healthy food profile is maintaining balance along with home-cooked meals (or at the very least, meals in which you know all of the ingredients). If cooking your own meals seems too daunting, remember that you can save a lot of time by batch-cooking several meals at once. Also, there are services that will help you automate or outsource the parts you don't like. For example, Blue Apron (www.blueapron.com) offers a service that effectively lets you automate meal planning and shopping. When you subscribe, they automatically send you a package containing all of the ingredients, recipes, and video instructions for three meals a week. Everything you need is delivered to you in the correct portions, so you don't have to try to figure out what to make or remember to buy the ingredients. All you have to do is cook it.

As you work toward optimizing your life and wellness, remember that there is no "one size fits all" for fitness and nutrition. No book can tell you the perfect solution that's ideally suited to you, but think of these guidelines as a really good place to start.

If you want to dig deeper into your diet, get a blood test from InsideTracker (www.insidetracker.com) and see where you're lacking. After arranging for blood work to be done, InsideTracker provides you with a dashboard on yourself. It tracks dozens of markers, from cholesterol to creatine kinase to testos-terone. It will also make specific nutritional recommendations and customized meal plans to help you reach your goals. You can track and monitor the results over time and view your progress.

To understand more, you can listen to my podcast interview with the founder of InsideTracker. If you use code ARIMTM10512, you can receive a discount on any of their plans.

So there you have it: fitness, sleep, and nutrition interact together to deter-mine your level of wellness. If you eat more, you need to work out more and sleep more. If you eat less, you can work out less and sleep less. If you sleep less, you need to work out less and eat less. If you work out more, you need to sleep more and eat more.

The truth is, if you eat a perfect diet and sleep a lot, you won't ever have to work out to maintain a good-looking, responsive body as long as you make a conscious effort to move on a daily basis (such as standing at your desk, taking the stairs instead of the elevator, and walking most places).

If it isn't clear yet, sleep is the big one. So, if you decide to train for a marathon, you're going to have to sleep more. You may not be ready to give up hours in the day for sleep—it's a choice you'll have to make. I have a nine-month-old son—if we have a bad night and I don't get to sleep well, I can't work out the next day because it will only be to my detriment. Good luck finding your optimal balance!

Conclusion

I really hope you've enjoyed this book. You've made a commitment to optimize, automate, and outsource everything in your life. I hope you dive into the deep end and try out the tools and techniques in these lectures.

For future updates and information, make sure to check out my blog and sign up for the newsletter.

I offer courses, corporate programs, and individual coaching to help anyone become more effective at everything. Please get in touch if you'd like to discuss how I can help. Feel free to contact me at: www.lessdoing.com/contact.

Good luck and thank you!

—Ari

Resources

Any time you need more help or just a refresher, you can sign up for my Udemy course on Less Doing. I also encourage you to check out my comprehensive course, "Making Gmail the Ultimate Productivity Tool," and my free course on IFTTT.

The Art of Less Doing Course

You can enhance your experience with interaction, collaboration, and guidance by enrolling in the Art of Less Doing course. You can go to www.lessdoing.com/learn to find out more.

Though it's not required, I highly recommend taking my other courses on Udemy as well:

- Making Gmail the Ultimate Productivity Tool: www.udemy.com/lessdoinggmail
- Automate and Outsource Your World with IFTTT and VAs: www.udemy.com/lessdoingifttt

Achievement Architecture—Be More Effective at Everything

Achievement Architecture is a coaching service that I've developed through a long process of experimentation, analytics, and personal tracking. Through Achievement Architecture, I've helped individuals achieve some amazing results. Anything you want to achieve is possible through building the right architecture—that is, the setting of goals. This includes everything from more productive corporate operations to treating chronic illnesses and even running a faster mile.

Anything is possible with the right analysis, tools, and methods provided in an Achievement Architecture coaching session. I am a problem solver. See my TED Talk on overcoming a seemingly insurmountable problem. I have worked with clients to:

- Take a startup from idea to reality with bare-bones resources

- Overcome chronic illness, sleep less, and other bio-hacking

- Go from running a 9.5-minute mile to a seven-minute mile in sixty days with no more than twenty minutes of daily exercise

- Go completely paperless, reclaim their inbox, and get back their time

- Outsource everything from virtual assistants and web developers to private investigators and composers

You can learn more at: www.lessdoing.com.

LessDoing.com

LessDoing.com started in early 2011 as a blog of productivity hacks. It quickly developed into a framework for optimizing, automating, and outsourcing everything in people's personal and professional lives. The blog covers everything from e-mail management to fitness, and helps make life easier. I encourage you to check out the blog and subscribe to the RSS feed, newsletter, and podcast.

The 80/20 Rule

Self-tracking and awareness: know where you are allocating resources so you can find areas to improve efficiency.

- RescueTime: http://bit.ly/1b9DAyl
- Basis: http://bit.ly/HHRkJ3
- FitBit: http://amzn.to/HuCoOE
- iDoneThis: http://bit.ly/1b9E8ET
- TimeHop: http://bit.ly/HuCAxn
- Thryve Food Tracker: http://bit.ly/1b2Nzcu
- Creating the "Manual of You": http://bit.ly/HuD8DB
- Essential vs. Optional: http://bit.ly/1cCz3LZ

Creating an "External Brain"

Create a note-taking system that is archived, searchable, and shareable. Stop prioritizing and get rid of your to-do list by working on your timing.

- E-mail and to-do lists: http://bit.ly/18Wsbkx

- FollowUp.cc: http://bit.ly/17DweZ6

- Evernote: http://bit.ly/1hKHTXN

- IFTTT (If This, Then That): http://ift.tt/186I759

- HassleMe: http://bit.ly/19zwgiU

- Re:snooze: http://bit.ly/1b5jrLU

- AquaNotes: http://amzn.to/1hKIys8

- WriteThat.Name: http://bit.ly/16DCddr

- The Evolution of the Virtual Assistant: http://bit.ly/1cCAeeg

- Zirtual: http://bit.ly/1iKKSO5

- Fancy Hands: http://bit.ly/1iKKZZo

- TalkTo: http://bit.ly/17Dx2gt

Customization

Solve problems with custom solutions.

- Indochino: http://bit.ly/1hKJ35t

- Youbars: http://bit.ly/175yCSo

- Vitamins on Demand: http://bit.ly/186mAIJ

- Elance: http://bit.ly/1cCAyd4

- Fiverr: http://bit.ly/HHU7IK

- Shapeways: http://bit.ly/19zySNL

Choose Your Own Workweek

Create a time period when certain activities will get done.

- ScheduleOnce: http://bit.ly/1gEkbLI

- RightInbox: http://bit.ly/1a5RVhX

Stop Running Errands

Errands are not efficient. Stop doing them.

- Amazon Subscribe & Save: http://amzn.to/HETtX9

- Amazon Prime: http://amzn.to/17DxECR

- Amazon Lockers: http://amzn.to/1apRNqi

- TaskRabbit: http://bit.ly/1gpCW7G

- RedBeacon: http://bit.ly/1egWNFn

- ShopRunner: http://bit.ly/1iKMITX

- Uber: http://bit.ly/1b9HYhe

Finances

Apply the 80/20 Rule to finances to get a handle on where your money is going.

- Mint: http://bit.ly/18WwiNo

- OneReceipt: http://bit.ly/HHWswQ

- BillGuard: http://bit.ly/16DF465

- FileThis: http://bit.ly/16DF4TD

- Square Reader: http://bit.ly/1fhFEZO

- Invisible Hand: http://bit.ly/19zBNGf

- SignNow: http://bit.ly/HHWvZv

Organization

Set limits and work within them to be more efficient.

- Dropbox: http://bit.ly/17DyTIy

- SortMyBox: http://bit.ly/1egYHWu

Batching

Group similar tasks together to gain momentum, like making meals or handling e-mails.

- Shoeboxed: http://bit.ly/HHWHbr
- Go Paperless: http://bit.ly/1aCZkbi

Wellness

Fitness, sleep, nutrition, and supplements

- CrossFit: http://bit.ly/HEVv9q
- The Fitness Triad: http://bit.ly/HEVAtU
- Grass-fed butter: http://bit.ly/1gpEMFm
- Good Fats: http://bit.ly/HEVMt4
- Blue-blocking sunglasses: http://amzn.to/1b9J3pb
- Blue Apron: http://bit.ly/1hh1e57
- InsideTracker: http://bit.ly/1hKMoBB
- Azumio Stress Doctor: http://bit.ly/1iKOfnv
- Krill oil: http://amzn.to/1b2UzpO
- Probiotics: http://amzn.to/19zECqP
- MCT oil (medium-chain triglycerides): http://bit.ly/1eh1yyy

ACKNOWLEDGMENTS

I would like to thank my parents, Louis and Susan, for their unwavering support throughout my life. My mother-in-law, Elisabeth, is no longer with us, but continues to be a guiding light for me every day.

Of course, this book would not have been made possible if not for a chance meeting between my editor, Andrew Yackira, and me. It has been a pleasure working with him, and I hope to make the Tarcher imprint proud.

SELF-HELP / PRODUCTIVITY

BELLEVILLE PUBLIC LIBRARY

3 1000 00334187 5

Less is more—or, more specifically, the less , the more life you have to live. Efficiency expert Ari Meisel details his "Less Doing" philosophy to streamline your life and make everything easier.

In our business and personal lives, it often seems as if the only way to get more done is by putting in more time—more hours at the office, more days running errands. But what if there was a way that we could do less, and free up more time for the things and people we love? If this sounds like what you need, Ari Meisel—TEDx speaker, efficiency consultant, and achievement architect—has the program for you. In *Less Doing, More Living*, Meisel explores the fundamental principles of his "Less Doing" philosophy, educating you on:

» Optimizing workflow with twenty-first-century apps and tools

» Creating an "external brain" in the Cloud to do all of your "lower" thinking—
like keeping track of appointments, meetings, and ideas

» Using technology to live a paper-free life

» The three fundamentals of wellness—fitness, sleep, and nutrition—
and technological approaches to improving these areas of life

» And much more

This book gives you new tools and techniques for streamlining your workload, being more efficient in your day-to-day activities, and making everything in life easier.

Ari Meisel has turned his hobby—optimizing productivity—into a popular framework and consulting service for automating and outsourcing life's tasks. His Less Doing philosophy continues to grow in popularity and has become a platform for general efficiency consulting to businesses, entrepreneurs, and others who could use a little more time in their lives. He lives on Long Island with his wife, their three children, and two dogs.

Visit the author's website at: **lessdoing.com**

U.S. **$15.95**/CAN $17.

JEREMY P. TARCHER/PENGUIN
a member of
Penguin Group (USA)
penguin.com

1404

Cover design by Dave Walker

Photograph of the author ©Deborah Kalas

Visit our website at:
tarcherbooks.com

ISBN 978-0-399-16852-9

51595

EAN 9 780399 168529